The ART
OF THE
PAPERWEIGHT —

Challenging Tradition

THE ART OF THE PAPERWEIGHT—

Challenging Tradition

Lawrence H. Selman, Guest Curator

PARTICIPATING MUSEUMS

The Art Museum of Santa Cruz County
Santa Cruz, California

Muscatine Art Center
Muscatine, Iowa

Jones Museum of Glass and Ceramics
Douglas Hill, Maine

Villa Terrace Museum of the Decorative Arts
Milwaukee, Wisconsin

Paperweight Press, 1993
Santa Cruz, California

This exhibition was organized by The Art Museum of Santa Cruz County
and is sponsored in part by
L. H. Selman Ltd. and the International Paperweight Society.

LENDERS TO THE EXHIBITION

Special thanks to the following collectors for lending pieces to this exhibit:

Jerold Gard, Charles Gaylord, Daniel MacLeith, Jack Narbutt,

L. H. Selman Ltd., Lawrence H. Selman, Debbie Tarsitano-Stankard

and various anonymous lenders

INQUIRIES

L. H. Selman Ltd.
761 Chestnut Street
Santa Cruz, California 95060
800 538-0766

©1993 Paperweight Press
Library of Congress Catalog Card Number: 93-087042
ISBN: 0-933756-18-6

CONTENTS

PREFACE

The Art of the Paperweight—Challenging Tradition is an intimate, inviting exhibition which The Art Museum of Santa Cruz County is pleased to share with our public. Upon entering the gallery, a microscopic world of miniature proportions emerges. Within this intimate environment, the visitor's eyes gaze upon clusters of millefiori, then a single flower draws their attention, then a kaleidoscope of color, on to a landscape; so it goes, on and on.

We are deeply grateful to our guest curator, Lawrence Selman, for gathering together this magical world of spheres and forms which have been captured in time and space. Larry, one of the world's most renowned paperweight authorities, has been a student, teacher and connoisseur of the paperweight art form for more than twenty-three years. We are grateful for the endless hours he has devoted to selecting this exhibition, and for creating the beautiful catalogue which accompanies it. Larry and Marti, his wife and partner, are long time residents of our community; our Museum is the fortunate beneficiary of their time, talent and resources. We appreciate the grant of funds from the International Paperweight Society and L. H. Selman Ltd. that made this exhibition possible. Also, we wish to acknowledge the special efforts of the staff at L. H. Selman Ltd., who contributed to its success.

No exhibition is complete without the cooperation and generosity of collectors who willingly lend their treasures for our viewing pleasure. Thank you to all those who contributed. I want to compliment Kathleen Moodie on another exceptional installation, and to recognize her contributions as a curator as she steadily assumes a greater share of the curatorial responsibilities for our Museum.

Once again, the Museum's volunteer council and staff deserve recognition and credit for their continued excellent performance.

Charles Hilger
Executive Director

FOREWORD

When paperweights were produced in the mid-nineteenth century, the format offered artisans their first opportunity to completely explore the decorative properties of glass. Until this time glasswork was limited to stricter utilitarian forms, such as vases, drinking vessels and pressed ware, which inhibited the glassworker from testing the true limits of glass.

In the beginning, the French factories probably intended these glass jewels to be used as paperweights; however it is doubtful that they ever were. Glass artisans quickly discovered the potential of the spherical format and exploited it to produce something that was worth much more than an object to hold down paper. The results of the Victorian's experimentation have had an impact that can be seen in almost every piece of art glass produced today.

The pieces in this exhibit were chosen because they demonstrate the way the paperweight artists of today and yesterday have significantly challenged the traditional boundaries of glass art. These paperweights display revolutionary uses of the glass medium. Glassworking of this quality has always been produced by rare talents, and today only a handful of artists possess the ability to produce pieces of this caliber. In order to make even the simplest paperweight, the glass artist must employ a range of skills far beyond the usual glassblowing techniques. Paperweight making is a highly competitive art form, with artists constantly driven to test the limits of glass, skill and imagination.

In 1966 Paul Jokelson published a book entitled *One Hundred of the Most Important Paperweights.* Part of the enjoyment of this book lay in the discussions it sparked: Why did the author choose this one? Why was this piece not included? Our hope is that this exhibit will spark similar debates. Through these discussions, perhaps we will all gain a better appreciation of this special art form.

Perhaps Truman Capote best described the power of these pieces when he said, "These objects were rather like frozen snowflakes, dazzling patterns frozen forever." I think you will agree, we have gathered some fabulous pieces for this exhibit, *The Art of the Paperweight—Challenging Tradition.*

Larry Selman

Lawrence H. Selman
Guest Curator

THE TRADITION

In 1845—little more than fifty years after a mob beheaded Louis XIV and proclaimed the land a republic—the great glass factories of France began to produce pieces of crystal that would permanently impact the history of glass art.

Paperweights—for that was their original purpose—were initially produced as novelty items for sale to a burgeoning middle class. The pieces received an instant enthusiastic response. The factories of Baccarat, Saint Louis and Clichy strived to surpass each other, and what was first sold as a novelty item metamorphosed into a presentation piece. When nations were called to display their finest accomplishments at London's Great Exhibition of 1851, paperweights were among the items France exhibited.

In Europe, it was the height of the Romantic Era—the works of Hugo, Baudelaire and Rousseau captivated the minds of a generation. Beethoven's symphonies were scarcely forty years old. The paperweight absorbed the romantic sensibilities of the people; their love of nature, their passionate desire for freedom and their appetite for greatness. The rise of industry was driven by a conviction that man could accomplish anything, and the idea that each individual had control of his own destiny was gradually becoming accepted.

In the years from 1845 to 1860, the government of France transformed from a monarchy to a republic to an empire. It is perhaps no coincidence that the majority of dated paperweights were produced in 1848, the year the people chose to liberate themselves from the rule of King Louis Philippe. The tricolor of the revolution—red for the spilled blood of patriots, white for their purity and virtue, and blue for their vigilance, were very real symbols to the people of France and one finds these colors abundantly displayed in paperweights, which absorbed these tenants capturing the passions and hopes of a generation in crystal.

Glass paperweights may be divided into three basic types—sulphide, millefiori, and lampwork.

Inspired by Roman art, sulphides were the first serious paperweights produced. These white clay cameo reliefs immortalized famous persons and events under crystal domes. In an era when photography and television were nonexistent, these startlingly realistic renditions of people and places served as a record of important figures and historical events.

A careful study of these pieces reveals the shift in cultural attitudes that occurred as France evolved. When Napoleon reigned, the French bourgeoisie saw themselves as the successors to the Romans, and they sought to emulate their civilization. In Napoleon's sulphide, the emperor has no beard. Just like the Romans, the French bourgeoisie viewed the beard as a characteristic of peasants and slaves and went clean shaven. Napoleon III's sulphide, however, portrays him with a beard—an accouterment that reflects the rise in popularity and a shift in focus towards the common man.

Millefiori weights, incorporating a glassworking technique that has been traced back to ancient Egypt, are composed of numerous glass canes. The term "millefiori" which translates from Italian as "thousand flowers" is aptly applied to these canes which, when arranged close together, often resemble "all the sorts of flowers which clothe the meadows in spring."[1]

Millefiori canes are composed of colorful patterns and pictures so incredibly minute, it is hard to understand how they are made. The secret to this art is the ductile quality of hot glass which allows the artist to create a pattern in large size and then shrink it until it appears as delicate and complex as a snowflake. To create a millefiori cane, the artist pours hot glass into a mold to create a shape, say a star. The glass is removed from the mold at a temperature where it retains the star shape, but it is still quite elastic. The glass holds its shape as the artist stretches it by the ends, but it reduces the star shape in diameter. By grouping several canes and fusing them together, the artist is able to form complex canes. As one can imagine, the process is extremely delicate and takes some time to master.

Lampwork, the last traditional style of paperweight making, is named for the oil lamps the Victorian glassworkers used to heat the glass rods they formed into fanciful and realistic portrayals of flowers, fruits and animals. Antique lampwork paperweights mostly portray fanciful stylized images—flowers more vibrant than any found in nature, and butterflies with all the colors of the rainbow on their wings. By their form, these pieces pay homage to the beauty of nature, but they also display an ambition to produce something finer than what one might actually find in nature. It is up to the individual to decide if the Victorian glass artists actually accomplished this feat. All these pieces are symptomatic of a period of time when man began to challenge what was commonly accepted as the limits of his skill.

Almost every lampwork motif bore some symbolism in the Victorian era, where it was common to communicate messages and sentiments with flowers. Paperweights displayed the most popular flowers of the day. The rose, pansy, primrose, convolvulus, fuchsia, wheatflower, chamomile and clematis were arranged in bouquets or singly with a garland of millefiori. It would be impossible for the French to ignore the obvious meanings of these blooms, many of which are still known today. The rose was a symbol of love, the pansy a symbol of remembrance, wheatflowers were presented to bring good luck. Some paperweights were specially commissioned and they can be found with inscriptions, sometimes a message of love or congratulations from the sender.

The encasement process (the act of placing a crystal dome over the internal motif), complicates the paperweight process tenfold. The internal motif must be kept heated at a temperature close to that of the gather (the molten crystal that will make up the dome) or it will crack and break. Joining two pieces of glass is an extremely delicate process; for each successful paperweight an artist is able to complete several are destroyed. The reward comes in the finished piece. Everything seems brighter and more alive underneath the sparkling crystal. As light fills the piece, an almost magical transformation occurs. The dome magnifies the internal subject matter in fascinating ways. Sometimes faceting multiplies the internal subject to create an amazing illusion. The dome format evokes themes of objectivity, timelessness and permanency. Indeed, unlike

---

[1] This comparison is first attributed to Marc Antonio Sabellico in *De Situ Urbis Venetae,* Book III, 1490's

paintings of the period, the color of a paperweight shows with the same brilliance as on the day it was created 150 years ago. The internal motif possesses the same unfathomable timelessness of an insect trapped in amber.

The art of the paperweight was also taken up at small glassworks in the areas surrounding France, including Italy, Bohemia and Silesia. As the paperweight's popularity grew, the art form was carried across the water to England and then the United States, where glass companies such as the Sandwich Glass Company, the New England Glass Company and the Mount Washington Glass Works interpreted the classic themes.

In the 3,500 years since man first produced glass, paperweights stand out as one of the glassmaker's most beautiful creations. Many of the techniques used to make the original French masterpieces have been lost. Even through endless experimentation, it has proved impossible to reproduce many of the colors achieved in the classic period. With paperweights, the classic-era glassworker issued a challenge to the modern glass artist: exceed my artistry, surpass my passion, eclipse this beauty.

ANTIQUE PAPERWEIGHTS

1. Magnum with cabbage rose and buds, furnace work with lampwork, Mount Washington Glass Company, ca. 1870–1890, diameter 4 3/8". This Mount Washington rose displays a wonderful dimensionality and a keen understanding of the anatomy of the plant. Deming Jarves, the enterprising merchant who also founded the New England Glass Company and the Sandwich Glass Company, started the Mount Washington Glass Company in South Boston in 1837. The glassworks quickly became known as a producer of the finest art glass. Mount Washington paperweights, virtuoso displays of skill, command higher prices than any other antique American paperweights.

2. Pink anemone, furnace work with lampwork, Pantin, ca. 1870–1880, diameter 3 1/8". To the Victorians, the anemone spoke of love forsaken, and one wonders what events might have surrounded the creation of this rare flower. This convincing portrayal displays a rare dimensionality and attention to detail.

3. Pink Blossom, furnace work with lampwork and millefiori, Clichy, ca. 1845–1860, diameter 2 7/8". Renowned among collectors, the Pink Blossom is a tribute to Clichy ingenuity, utilizing split millefiori canes to form the large open pink petals of the flower. The wonderfully realistic bud of the plant stands in stark contrast to the flower's fabulous stamens—each of which is a tiny white star.

4. Primrose, furnace work with lampwork and millefiori, Baccarat, ca. 1845–1860, diameter 3 1/16". The bloom of this flower is colored like a fiery sun, appropriate colors for a bloom that symbolized the coming warmth of spring. The artist emphasizes the lushness of the bloom by framing it within a seemingly informal tiara of verdant green leaves.

5. Wallflower, furnace work with lampwork and millefiori, Baccarat, ca. 1845–1860, diameter 3 1/16". Everyone is familiar with the term "wallflower", applied to the shy person at a dance who stands by the wall. Legend says the wallflower was once a woman who was killed when she fell from a tower wall as she attempted to elope against her father's wishes. Her love was so strong that she came back as this flower, and she continues to cling to stone walls, waiting for her lover. The glassworkers outdid themselves with this fantastic piece which embodies story and legend. To the Victorians this bloom spoke of fidelity in adversity. The unusual complex millefiori bud of this flower matches the cane found in the center of the bloom.

6. Pelargonium, furnace work with lampwork, Saint Louis, ca. 1845–1860, diameter 3 1/8". The delicate swirling white latticinio of this piece conjures the romantic image of a flower left on a bedspread coverlet, while the bloom itself speaks of an inclination for a permanent relationship.

7. Blue camomile with white bud, furnace work with lampwork and millefiori, Baccarat, ca. 1845–1860, diameter 2 3/8". For centuries, the camomile has been said to provide strength in adversity, and the star-cut ground in this piece creates the illusion that power is emanating from the bloom. A garland of red, white and blue canes around the exterior of the piece carries patriotic overtones. Each of the following examples of the popular camomile, display a different treatment of the same theme by a single factory.

8. Yellow camomile with red buds, furnace work with lampwork and millefiori, Baccarat, ca. 1845–1860, diameter 2 7/16". Baccarat cleverly composed the bloom of its camomile flowers by fusing C-shaped rods to a central millefiori cane, effectively forming a large complex cane. The unusual pair of bright red buds, placed strategically to offset the bloom, makes a splendid addition to this piece.

9. Rare copper camomile with red bud, furnace work with lampwork and millefiori, Baccarat, ca. 1845–1860, diameter 2 1/2". In this rare example of the camomile, convex faceting heightens the delicacy of the flower. Light bends as it hits the cutting, creating the illusion that two garlands of millefiori canes surround the flower. As one views the flower from different angles, he becomes mystified by the shimmering illusion created by the cutting on the dome.

10. Scarlet fuchsias, furnace work with lampwork, Pantin, ca. 1870–1880, diameter 3". This magnificent flower is an example of the brilliant color attained by nineteenth-century glassworkers. The gorgeous scarlet and blue blossoms display a remarkable intensity of color.

11. Fuchsias on swirling latticinio, furnace work with lampwork, Saint Louis, ca. 1845–1860, diameter 2 13/16". The fuchsia was first cultivated in European greenhouses during the early eighteen hundreds. The flower caught on almost immediately, becoming a status symbol among the bourgeoisie. The owner of a fuchsia was viewed as an extremely fashionable person with good taste. This painterly portrayal immortalizes the Victorian predilection for the flower.

12. Buttercup with millefiori garland, furnace work with lampwork and millefiori, New England Glass Company, ca. 1852–1880, diameter 2 7/16". Buttercups were imbued with the power to prophesize a coming romance. To emphasize this theme, the artisan enhanced the garland of millefiori surrounding the flower with a number of heart silhouettes. The pink ground is an unusual addition to this superb weight.

13. White rose with bud, furnace work with lampwork, attrib. Saint Louis or Baccarat, ca. 1845–1860, diameter 3". Victorian artisans achieved an attractive effect by placing this flower inside a dome of hollow crystal. The airspace gives the rose a wet, dewy appearance, conjuring images of a flower picked in the early morning sunlight. Perhaps Truman Capote described a similar piece when he wrote about his prized white rose weight: *"When it's a quarter to two and sleep hasn't come, a restfulness arises from contemplating a quiet white rose, until the rose expands into the whiteness of sleep."*

14. "Thousand-petaled" red rose, furnace work with lampwork, Baccarat, ca. 1845-1860, diameter 2 1/2". So called because of its numerous petals, the unmistakable splendor of the "thousand petaled" rose speaks of a love with boundless intensity. The blood-red color of the bloom alludes to the passion of the sender. This type of flower is also sometimes referred to as a cabbage rose because of its tightly furled petals.

15. Pink millefiori rose with bud, furnace work with lampwork and millefiori, Clichy, ca. 1845–1860, diameter 2 3/4". Clichy captured the imagination of the Victorian people with its millefiori rose cane, utilized here to form the bloom of a flower. This delicate cane, highly sought-after, embodies all the mystique and beauty of the real flower. In this rendition, the flower rests on a bed of delicate swirling latticinio, a rose in a spider web.

BOUQUETS

16. Posy with millefiori garland, furnace work with lampwork and millefiori, Saint Louis, ca. 1845–1860, diameter 3 1/4". Saint Louis artisans created this inventive bouquet by placing millefiori cane flowers on lampwork leaves and stalks. The millefiori garland surrounding the piece is multiplied so the viewer sees it three times. The gorgeous amber ground evokes the golden rays of a dramatic sunset.

17. Clear encased double overlay with upright bouquet, furnace work with lampwork and millefiori, Saint Louis, ca. 1845–1860, diameter 3 3/16". Clear encased double overlays of this type were produced by an extremely delicate process, and most shattered before reaching completion. The overlay, preserved eternally by a coat of clear crystal, frames the bouquet from the top, at the same time inviting one to explore the nooks and crannies of the three-dimensional bouquet from the sides. The gorgeous bouquet glows with the exotic beauty of some rare under-sea blossoms.

18. Faceted upright bouquet with spiraling filigree torsade, furnace work with lampwork and millefiori, Saint Louis, ca. 1845–1860, diameter 3 3/16". Faceting multiplies a spiraling red and white torsade to create the illusion that this fancy bouquet rests on an astonishingly delicate piece of lacework. A concrete example of Victorian sensibilities, this exquisite display merges the fineness of the products of industry and nature.

19. Multifloral bouquet, furnace work with lampwork, Saint Louis, ca. 1845–1860, diameter 3 3/16". A pelargonium sits at the center of an impromptu arrangement of flowers in this dazzling bouquet, which evokes all the emotions involved with picking flowers for a loved one. The amount of lampwork in bouquet weights made them extremely difficult to produce.

20. Three-flower bouquet with buds, furnace work with lampwork and millefiori, Clichy, ca. 1845–1860, diameter 2 7/8". Clichy was renowned for its inventive flower portrayals, no two of which are exactly alike. This bouquet appears to be tied with a knot on the right, a detail which signified the flowers were meant to ask a question of the recipient. For the person with a knowledge of Victorian flower language, the question becomes clear. The pansy asks if the recipient feels tenderly towards the sender, while the clematis flowers wish for a positive reply.

21. Bouquet with pansy and clematis blossoms, furnace work with lampwork and millefiori, Baccarat, ca. 1845–1860, diameter 3 1/16". Red, white and blue clematis blossoms with stardust centers are arranged with a large pansy in this patriotic bouquet. People used the pansy as a subtle way to show support for Napoleon and the empire after he was deposed.

22. Bouquet with central pink rose, furnace work with lampwork and millefiori, Clichy, ca. 1845–1860, diameter 2 3/4". Clichy artisans grouped an amazing range of flower forms in this bouquet to create an exquisite explosion of color. The tightly-gathered flowers, centered on the famous Clichy rose, are reminiscent of a delicate bridal bouquet.

23. Bouquet garland, furnace work with lampwork and millefiori, Saint Louis, ca. 1845–1860, diameter 2 3/4". The wonderful naiveté of this loose arrangement of blossoms evokes the carefree pleasures of a warm spring day. The informal garland of flowers conjures the image of a May Day celebration.

24. Magnum bouquet with pompon, clematis and pansies, furnace work with lampwork and millefiori, Baccarat, ca. 1845–1860, diameter 3 9/16". In contrast to the work of the other French factories, Baccarat produced conspicuously formal floral arrangements. These masterfully portrayed flowers combine to form a delightful garden. The millefiori cane sections that compose the bottom of the pansies indicate that this weight was produced in the early part of the classic period.

25. Magnum upright bouquet with clematis blossoms in a latticinio funnel basket, furnace work with lampwork and millefiori, New England Glass Company, ca. 1852–1880, diameter 4". Cherries and apples peek from beneath the leaves of gorgeous double clematis blossoms in this dazzling bouquet. While it might seem odd by today's standards, fruit was a common element of mid-nineteenth century bouquets. Mingling symbols of hope and fulfillment, this complex piece carries the upright bouquet theme to new heights.

FRUIT & VEGETABLES

26. Magnum with strawberries nestled in emerald leaves, furnace work with lampwork, Mount Washington Glass Company, ca. 1870–1890, diameter 3 7/8". This weight might have been inspired by the "strawberry fever" that swept the United States between 1858 and 1870, when new growing methods made the fruit readily available. The ripe berries take on a wonderful dimensionality in this piece, jumping out at the viewer from under the high magnification of the dome. To create the small seeds of the fruit, the artist painstakingly applied bits of glass to the surface of the berries, giving them a sugary sweet appearance that makes the mouth water.

27. Three ripe strawberries, furnace work with lampwork, Pantin, ca. 1870–1880, diameter 3 3/16". Artists have striven to pay homage to the beauty of the strawberry since Egyptian times. It is the first plant to blossom and bear fruit in the spring, and it has become closely associated with this season. The berry forms in this piece were created by coating lampworked white glass with translucent ruby. Light plays upon the dimensionality of the form, creating brilliant shading effects under the dome. What this fanciful depiction lacks in scientific accuracy is offset by its artistry. The dazzling portrayal is a piece of sheer visual poetry.

28. Strawberries on star-cut ground, furnace work with lampwork and millefiori, Baccarat, ca. 1845–1860, diameter 3 1/8". The artisans at Baccarat ingeniously fused hexagonal rods together to create the dimensional berries in this interpretation of the strawberry. This portrayal might seem inaccurate when compared with today's strawberry, but one must remember that the fruit we know is a hybrid developed over the past one hundred and fifty years. Commonly-found strawberries of the period more closely resembled this fruit, which was renowned for its sourness. In mid-nineteenth-century France, strawberries were presented as a gift to provide foresight.

29. Pear and cherries in latticinio funnel basket, furnace work with lampwork, Saint Louis, ca. 1845–1860, diameter 3 1/8". The scale of the fruits in this arrangement is portrayed more realistically than most of Saint Louis's fruit weights. The delicate latticinio ground has been pulled down to form a funnel-shaped basket for the fruit.

30. Hollow-blown apple on square crystal cushion, furnace work with glass blowing, Saint Louis, ca. 1845–1860, width at base 3 1/2". An excellent variation of the paperweight format, this apple is portrayed in high relief with no glass dome. Those familiar with the story of Adam and Eve know the apple symbolizes temptation, and perhaps this realistic interpretation of the fruit was crafted to provide a lesson about the iniquity to those who tried to eat it. If anything betrays the fruit's realism, it is that it appears to be too perfect. This piece later inspired the production of similar weights at the New England Glass Company.

31. Fruits in latticinio funnel basket, furnace work with lampwork, Saint Louis, ca. 1845–1860, diameter 3". Perhaps unique, this piece combines the lampwork normally found in two Saint Louis weights to form an extraordinary cornucopia. By studying the different leaf types in the piece, one discovers that Saint Louis artisans enhanced their normal portrayal of fruits in a basket with lampwork pieces from a cherry weight.

32. Turnips on latticinio, furnace work with lampwork, Saint Louis, ca. 1845–1860, diameter 2 13/16". Saint Louis artisans transformed a relatively unappealing and bland theme into a display of color and elegance with this turnip weight. The impulse to portray turnips probably stemmed from the virtue they symbolized—charity.

S W I R L S & C R O W N S

33. Crown with circlet of millefiori, furnace work with millefiori, Bohemia, ca. 1845–1860, diameter 2 3/4". If paperweights were created by a process of evolution, this piece would be placed somewhere in the middle of Clichy's swirl and Saint Louis's crown weights. The red and white spokes form a powerful setting for the delicate millefiori canes.

34. Three-color crown with latticinio spokes, furnace work with millefiori, Saint Louis, ca. 1845–1860, diameter 3 1/8". This piece, modeled upon a king's crown, carries all the elegance and refinement of the symbol of power. The precision with which the glassmaker placed the parts of the design together is a phenomenal demonstration of skill.

35. Latticinio crown, furnace work with millefiori, New England Glass Company, ca. 1852–1880, diameter 2 1/2". New England Glass Company artisans achieved a completely different effect with this crown, which is composed almost entirely of delicate lace filigree. Lace was a popular decorative element of the Victorian era, a cloth associated with elegance and grace. When glassworkers sought to imitate its fineness they began a new form of glassworking—one that has been difficult to emulate in modern times.

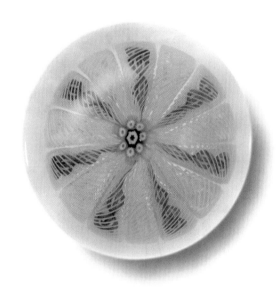

36. Miniature swirl with pink and green rose, furnace work with millefiori, Clichy, ca. 1845–1860, diameter 1 3/4". Clichy artisans were keenly aware of the optical properties of crystal, and they exploited them to the fullest in their swirl weights. Under the magnification of the dome, whirling millefiori pinwheels create a scintillating visual illusion, forming a dramatic ground for the millefiori cane. This piece holds one spellbound, a twisting whirlpool with a rose at its center.

37. Close packed panels of millefiori divided with red and white twists, furnace work with millefiori, Saint Louis, ca. 1845–1860, diameter 2 13/16". Saint Louis used spiraling twists to divide this weight into pie-shaped panels. This piece appears as a colorful ball of flowers wrapped with a red and white ribbon.

38. Close packed millefiori in green and white stave basket, furnace work with millefiori, Clichy, ca. 1845–1860, diameter 3 1/16". The French factories included their most spectacular millefiori canes in close packed weights. Many of the canes in this piece possess a snowflake-like fineness that can only be seen with a magnifying glass. In this piece, the artisans pulled down an outer row of canes to create the illusion of a basket filled with an informal arrangement of fanciful blooms. A blue and white garland of pastry-mold canes frames the millefiori arrangement.

39. Extremely rare and important triple weight, furnace work with lampwork and millefiori, Baccarat, ca. 1845–1860, diameter 2 1/2". This piece exemplifies the spirit of competition between the French factories. In an attempt to outdo their rivals, Baccarat artisans fused three paperweights together to create this *tour de force*. The process to create such a piece involved technical skill few must have possessed. This imaginative piece exhibits the commanding presence of a king on a chess board.

BASKETS

40. Close packed piedouche, furnace work with millefiori, Clichy, ca. 1845–1860, height 2 7/16", diameter 3". The piedouche was another innovative variation of the paperweight format. The artisans accentuated the grandeur of the millefiori by literally placing it on a pedestal. These pieces are also known as basket weights, because they conjure poetic images of a bright basket filled with *"a thousand flowers."* All of the major French factories produced pedestal weights, but Clichy excelled in this area. The colors of the canes in this piece have been toned down to soft, flowery pastels.

41. Mushroom bouquet, furnace work with millefiori, Clichy, ca. 1845–1860, diameter 2 3/4". Clichy artisans paid homage to the beauty of the bouquet in this piece, which contains six rows of concentric complex canes. An outer row of canes has been pulled down to form a pink and white sheath for this splendid formal arrangement. Concave faceting accentuates the fineness of the bouquet. Mushroom bouquets are among the most beautiful and technically challenging weights produced during the classic period.

WAR & REVOLUTION

42. Millefiori fireworks, furnace work with millefiori, Baccarat, ca. 1845–1860, diameter 2 15/16". In this patriotic piece, the artisans formed the design by placing spaced rows of millefiori rods on a vertical slant. The spaces between the rows of millefiori cause the tops of the canes to take on the appearance of exploding fireworks. The ridged sides of the rods add a sense of motion to the piece, and as one studies it he can almost hear the screaming rockets that heralded a new hope for the French people.

43. Letter press with sulphide of Marie Joseph de Chenier, furnace work with cameo encrustation, Baccarat, ca. 1838–1860, 3 1/16" x 6". Marie Joseph de Chenier was one of the French revolutionaries responsible for the overthrow of Louis XIV and Marie Antoinette. Ironically, the revolution also meant the death of Chenier's brother on the scaffold. His somber features capture all the pain and glory of the first French revolution.

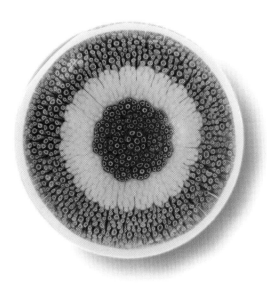

44. Tricolor carpet ground, furnace work with millefiori, Saint Louis, ca. 1845–1860, diameter 2 13/16". A piece of history made solid, this weight conjures the same emotion one feels when viewing the original revolutionary flags. The simple red, white and blue canes embody the passions and hopes of a generation. There is something special about this piece, whose colors show with the same patriotic fervor as on the day it was made.

CARPET GROUNDS

45. Carpet ground with dancing man, dancing woman, devil and horses, furnace work with millefiori, Saint Louis, ca. 1845–1860, diameter 2 7/16". A sea of pale green cog canes serves as an elegant setting for five silhouette canes in this remarkable weight. Most striking is the dramatic pose of each of the figures. In other weights, the dancing man and woman are often found together in the same cane, where their poses intimate popular dances of the period. Separated in this piece, the man appears as though he is about to deliver a soliloquy of longing, while the lonely woman, with out-stretched arms, yearns for her partner. The devil seems sure to be up to mischief.

46. Interlaced trefoil garlands on white stardust carpet ground, furnace work with millefiori, Baccarat, ca. 1845–1860, diameter 3". This refined piece reminds the viewer of formally arranged flowers planted in a garden of white stones. The complex blue and red arrow canes in the center of each loop take on the appearance of bubbling fountains.

47. Spaced millefiori on moss carpet ground with prairie canes, furnace work with millefiori, Clichy, ca. 1845–1860, diameter 2 1/16". Clichy utilized its moss ground in this weight to create the illusion of vibrant wildflowers on a green lawn. It is an extraordinary example of the factory's color vocabulary, including shades of ruby, pink, thalo blue, turquoise, cadmium green and Naples yellow.

LACE & GARLANDS

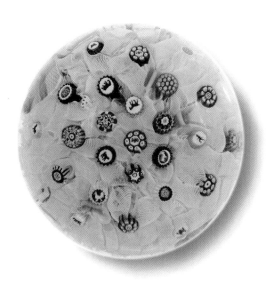

48. Magnum spaced millefiori Gridel on lace, furnace work with millefiori, Baccarat, dated 1847, diameter 4". In 1847, Joseph Emil Gridel, the nine-year-old nephew of Baccarat manager Jean-Baptiste Toussaint, cut eighteen different animals out of paper. The designs soon became models for millefiori silhouette canes. The fanciful shadow figures tantalize the viewer, imbuing millefiori with the romance of the swan, lovebirds and butterfly, and importing the exotic figures of the monkey, elephant and camel. Other figures, such as the deer, squirrel, rooster, devil, dog, horse and goat carry their own appeal. This enormous weight, dated to indicate it was one of the first Gridel weights produced, is a masterful demonstration of these canes. Gridel, coincidentally, grew up to become a famous painter of animal life.

49. Scattered millefiori on lace with a "j" cane, furnace work with millefiori, Bohemian, dated 1848, diameter 3 1/8". In this magnificent piece, millefiori canes have been scattered across white lace to appear as wildflowers pushing their heads up through melting snow. Few of these mysterious signed "j" weights are known to exist. Its canes display a fineness and coloring that rivals its French counterparts. It is unknown whether the lowercase "j" by the date indicates a factory name or is an abbreviation of the German word for year ("Jahr"). Silhouette canes abound and one finds, among other things, a patriotic rendition of the Austrian crowned eagle and multicolored bees.

50. C-scroll garland on lace, furnace work with millefiori, Clichy, ca. 1845–1860, diameter 3 1/8". Clichy cleverly signed this paperweight by creating a garland composed of C-shaped crescents. The crescents form the petals of an abstract flower shape around the concentric circles of millefiori in the center of the piece. Garland weights have an especially effective impact on a lace ground, which sets off the canes like brilliant jewels.

51. Cinquefoil garland on lace with Gridel silhouettes, furnace work with millefiori, Baccarat, ca. 1845–1860, diameter 3 1/8". Glassworkers formed this ingenious garland by combining five question mark-shaped loops of canes to form a star-shaped pattern. The silhouettes imbue the piece with drama and symbolism. For example, it is easy to visualize the butterfly fluttering among the millefiori flowers. After the first revolution, the French proudly characterized themselves with the rooster, a symbol that exemplified the vigilance of the people against tyranny.

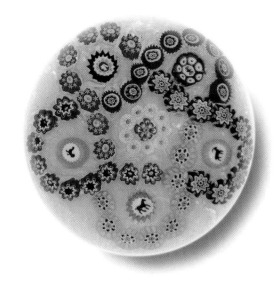

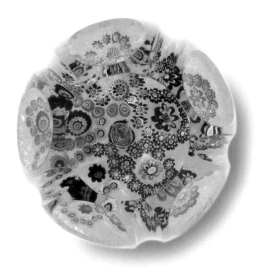

52. Faceted cinquefoil garland with central pink and green rose, furnace work with millefiori, Clichy, ca. 1845–1860, diameter 3 1/8". Faceting in this piece alters the garland so it takes on a mirage-like quality. As one turns the weight, florets shimmer around a central pink rose.

53. Circular garlands with large central pink and green rose, furnace work with millefiori, Clichy, ca. 1845–1860, diameter 3 1/4". With its rich turquoise ground, this piece conjures images of flowers floating on the surface of a clear blue pond. Green cog canes take on the role of lily pads, while the bold central rose cane is suggestive of a large pink lotus (a flower identified in the nineteenth century as *Rosae Plena*, also renowned for the remarkable size it achieves). The formal circular garlands of millefiori flowers evoke the movement of ripples in the water.

54. Patterned millefiori surrounding the initials "D" and "P", furnace work with millefiori, Clichy, ca. 1845–1860, diameter 3 1/16". This piece, containing the initials, "D" and "P", is obviously a special order. Perhaps it was presented as a wedding gift to the Duchess of Parma on the day she married in 1845. Wondering at the events surrounding its creation imbues the piece with a special romance.

55. Green snake coiled on lace cushion, furnace work with lampwork, Baccarat, ca. 1845–1860, diameter 2 7/8". Baccarat artisans merged two images of elegance with this portrayal of a snake on a lace cushion. One wonders what story lies behind its construction. The lace causes one to think that the piece belonged to a woman, or that it was meant to characterize a woman. *Femme fatale*—the idea of the female being alluring, yet possessing a painful bite was a popular image in art and poetry at the time. Or, perhaps this is a representation of the serpent who tempted Eve. The entire presentation is masterfully put together. In bright light, brilliant prisms form in the facets. As one turns the piece in his hands, the geometric cuts impart a sense of movement to the snake's head.

56. Butterfly with millefiori garland, furnace work with lampwork, Baccarat, ca. 1845–1860, diameter 3 3/16". Baccarat glassworkers adroitly flattened millefiori canes to create the wings of their thrilling butterflies. These insects dazzle the viewer, the delicate archetypes of a vibrant imagination. The millefiori garland forms a decorative frame of flowers around the colorful insect.

57. Butterfly hovering over pansy, furnace work with lampwork, Baccarat, ca. 1845–1860, diameter 3 1/8". The addition of a pansy below the butterfly transforms this piece into a marvelous three-dimensional scene. This compound layering effect is an advanced demonstration of skill.

After the classic period, for a number of economic reasons, paperweight production gradually declined. Beginning in the early twentieth century, a strong field of collectors began to search out pieces of the prized glasswork. As early as 1939, writer Ruth Webb Lee noted in an article, "Paperweights are distinctly the fad of the moment." Demand for antique paperweights continued to rise, causing prices for the complex pieces of glasswork to soar.

Even so, in 1950 modern paperweight making was still a lost art. Many of the advanced skills used in making antique paperweights were lost. During this period several events occurred that sparked a modern renaissance of paperweight making. Paul Jokelson, a shipping magnate and longtime collector of paperweights, played a key role in several of these events. First, he formed the Paperweight Collector's Association—a group that brought collectors together to learn about paperweights. Next, he prodded Baccarat and Saint Louis to begin to rediscover the old weight-making skills. Jokelson, along with several other collectors (most notable of these was Evangeline Bergstrom), published several books that made information about paperweights readily available to new collectors. This information also inspired studio glass artists across America to experiment with making paperweights. Among the most successful of these pioneers was Charles Kaziun of Brockton, Massachusetts, whose work many say rivals the antiques.

While many of the skills used to make the antique paperweights remain a mystery, experimentation has sparked a modern renaissance of paperweight production. Today, modern glass artists have acquired new skills and discovered techniques that place their work on a par of excellence with the antiques.

The Victorian glassworker was limited by the technology of the day. He fashioned paperweights over a wood fire using relatively crude tools. The rigorous demands of working with glass made teamwork an imperative part of glassworking, and paperweights were only produced in factories. With the advent of modern technology, artists found they no longer had to work as part of a factory to produce paperweights. Working in a small studio with a furnace or torch fueled by natural gas or propane, the glassworker gained independence to explore different styles and test new techniques. For many, the production of paperweights became a personal creative endeavor. The ability to work privately led to the production of pieces which contain personal reflections of the individual, such as Barry Sautner's *Soul in a Cage.* The benefits of technology also manifested in many factories, where artists were not only granted the freedom to explore glass on their own, but retained the ability to call on a fellow glassworker for advice.

The modern section of this catalogue begins with pieces which have been fundamental to the discovery of the lost art of paperweight making. Like the original French paperweights, these pieces portray stylized flowers and animals. They also exhibit the finest modern achievements in the art of millefiori and filigree. Of special note are Parabelle Glass' spectacular magnum basket and the Saint Louis newel post, which push the art of millefiori to its limits.

The next section displays paperweights which are modern interpretations of classic themes. These interpret the themes portrayed in antique weights with a new vision. For example, Rick Ayotte's Peace rose bouquet is the progression of Baccarat's "thousand-petaled" rose. Perthshire Paperweights' hollow weight with a giant panda finds inspiration in the antique hollow weight with the white rose.

The pieces in the final section of this catalogue demonstrate how the contemporary glass artist employs modern and classic techniques to create artwork with personal themes and novel formats. These include pieces such as Andrew Fote's *Silver Dreamer* and Rick Ayotte's *Ducks in the Pond,* which display innovative techniques and convey the influence of contemporary sensibilities.

Two distinct styles of work run throughout the catalogue. The first school of artists produces paperweights incorporating decorative qualities. These artists challenge tradition with imagination and their ability to manipulate glass. Their pieces are created according to the artist's own personal aesthetic, a sensibility which is oftentimes highly influenced by the nineteenth-century antiques. Many artists, such as Peter Raos and David Salazar, draw inspiration from poetry and art.

The other style of paperweight making is composed of artists who draw their inspiration directly from nature, attempting to create life-like glass flora and fauna. Paul Stankard pioneered this approach in paperweights with his portrayal of glass wildflowers—renditions that are so true to nature they incorporate leaves that have been nibbled by insects, and flowers that wilt from lack of water. Stankard portrays nature so convincingly that his flowers radiate vitality, and many a novice has been fooled into believing he incorporates real blooms into his work. While most admire such pieces simply for their beauty, they also evoke powerful themes through their portrayal of growth and decay.

Chris Buzzini, another artist who carries this style to new heights, portrays flowers that do not suffer the plagues of nature. His awe-inspiring representations display the award-winning beauty of the prized roses at a flower show. A number of artists, such as Rick Ayotte and Jim Donofrio, excel in their ability to transform glass into the illusion of animal life. While these artists strive for realism, their portrayals display stylistic variations caused by their screen of perception and the techniques they use to create their pieces. This artistic dimension sometimes strikes the most powerful chord in the viewer.

Many artists draw inspiration from both categories, combining the best qualities of each school of thought. A number of pieces, such as Debbie Tarsitano's *Cat in the Window, Rainy Afternoon* and Gordon Smith's *Ancestral Dream,* play upon modern sensibilities. Through cultural bonds, we share their perceptions and the pieces impact us more powerfully.

We are fortunate to live during the occurrence of a modern renaissance in the art of the paperweight. As we view the latest creations of the finest modern glassworkers, we understand the excitement the people of the mid-nineteenth century felt when they saw the latest creations of the classic-era French factories.

MODERN PAPERWEIGHTS

58. Magnum newel post, furnace work with millefiori, Saint Louis, dated 1993, height 8", diameter 4 9/16". In this masterful demonstration of cane work, Saint Louis glassworkers challenge the beauty of a renowned antique Baccarat newel post. Using traditional Saint Louis millefiori and silhouette canes, the glass artists have fashioned a globe which includes *"all the sorts of flowers which clothe the meadows in spring."*

59. Close packed millefiori with zodiac silhouettes, furnace work with millefiori, Baccarat, dated 1991, diameter 3 3/16". Baccarat glassworkers incorporated the myth of the zodiac in this presentation which features silhouettes of the twelve signs. The zodiac signs have become factory trademarks in modern times, much as the Gridels served in the nineteenth century. The millefiori in this piece, a combination of traditional and modern canes, display a delicate elegance.

60. One-of-a-kind modern triple weight, furnace work with millefiori, Parabelle Glass, dated 1993, height 4 1/4", diameter 3 1/8" at base. One of the key figures in the discovery of the lost weight making techniques, Gary Scrutton of Parabelle Glass outdoes himself with this talented display. In addition to rediscovering lost techniques, Parabelle has developed a wide array of imaginative new complex canes and glass colors. The cheerful pansy cane is a Parabelle trademark.

61. Magnum basket, furnace work with millefiori, Parabelle Glass, dated 1993, height 2 1/4", diameter 4".
This piece was inspired by a famous antique Clichy weight which sold for $258,000 in 1990—the highest price ever paid for a paperweight. This spectacular presentation captures the gaiety of a basket filled with flowers. Brightly-colored millefiori canes, including twenty-seven roses and fourteen pansies, appear close to the surface of the weight. White prairie canes set into the rich moss ground accent the millefiori like tiny white baby's breath.

62. Millefiori with gold-foil Masonic symbol, lampwork encasement with millefiori and gold inclusion, Charles Kaziun II, ca. 1960–1970, diameter 2 1/16".
Charles Kaziun is said to have produced many of his paperweights using a store of glass imported from France in 1880. In this weight, a robin's-egg blue ground is accented with delicate complex canes in emerald, aquamarine and ruby, which are arranged inside a spiraling pink, white and royal blue torsade. The entire piece gleams with a breathtaking, jewel-like quality.

63. Magnum three-color crown, furnace work with millefiori, dated 1991, diameter 3 15/16".
With 28 precisely-placed spokes, this piece rivals the most elaborate antique renditions of the crown. The weight sparkles with finesse, the multicolored spokes spiraling from a central complex cane like gay party streamers.

64. Blue marbrie design, furnace work with millefiori, Scott Beyers of Orient and Flume Art Glass, dated 1992, diameter 3 3/8". The marbrie pattern has been created since the first paperweights were produced. The design is thought to have been adapted from "witch balls", crystal globes which were hung in the doorways of medieval cottages to ward off evil spirits. In this modern interpretation, Scott Beyers carries the design to new heights of fineness.

65. Magnum lizard on sandy ground with aloe flower, lampwork encasement with lampwork, Victor Trabucco, dated 1993, diameter 4 3/4". The lizard, or salamander, is a mythical creature renowned for its ability to withstand extreme heat. According to tradition, the fabulous creature inhabits the glassworker's furnace and at certain times it issues from its abode to carry back a victim. In this paperweight, we find one of these creatures trapped in crystal. Victor Trabucco individually fused over 500 canes together to create the scales on the body of this imposing reptile, which draws inspiration from an antique Pantin weight.

66. Miniature blue blossom and bud, lampwork encasement with lampwork, David and Jon Trabucco, dated 1991, diameter 2". David and Jon Trabucco portray blossoms more perfect than one could find in nature with this bouquet of fantasy flowers, which features two different types of blossoms growing on the same stalk.

67. Saint Anne's clematis, lampwork encasement with lampwork and millefiori, Randall Grubb, dated 1993, diameter 3 1/16". Randall Grubb instills an old theme with modern artistry in this remake of an antique Baccarat garland weight. The piece depicts a classic motif—the double clematis over a star-cut ground. In this portrayal the vibrant scarlet petals of the flower radiate outward like flames, and Grubb includes a wonderful millefiori bud. The delicate outer garland of canes is composed of tiny stars and hearts.

68. Pink cabbage rose with spiral torsade, lampwork encasement with lampwork, Ray Banford, dated 1992, diameter 3". This rose was inspired by a rare weight produced at the Sandwich Glass Company in the late eighteen hundreds. Ray Banford combines delicate lampwork and filigree elements to form a stirring tribute to the rose.

69. Pink and lavender fuchsia, furnace work with lampwork, Perthshire Paperweights, dated 1993, diameter 3 1/8". The snowy lace ground beneath the flower increases the intensity of the colors in this vivid portrayal of the fuchsia. Perthshire glassworkers interpret the classic theme in their own style, portraying the flower with a crisp accuracy.

70. *Floral bouquet, lampwork encasement with lampwork and millefiori, Ken Rosenfeld, dated 1993, diameter 3 3/8".* Ken Rosenfeld is renowned for his bold use of color and inventive flower forms. This luxuriant flower garden was grown with the magic of a fertile imagination.

CLASSIC INTERPRETATIONS

71. *FLOWERS IN THE MEADOW magnum, lampwork encasement with lampwork and millefiori, Debbie Tarsitano, dated 1992, diameter 4 1/4".* For those who test the limits of glass by including extraordinary amounts of lampwork, the results can be astounding. This magnificent thirty-flower *tour de force* captures the splendor of a field of flowers. As an art object, it holds its own against any piece of glass ever created.

72. *SPRINGTIME ORCHARD magnum, lampwork encasement with lampwork, Randall Grubb, dated 1993, diameter 4 11/16".* Randall Grubb outdoes himself with this portrayal of a branch with over thirty delicate pink apple blossoms and buds nestled in jade-colored, antique-style leaves. The realistic flowers combine with the jewel-like leaves to form a spectacular effect.

73. Upright pink Peace rose, Illusion Series, lampwork encasement with lampwork, Rick Ayotte, dated 1993, diameter 3". The Peace rose is a hybrid flower developed after World War I to suggest the promise of a world without war—where people could live together in harmony and love. Ayotte immortalizes these sentiments in this realistic portrayal of the flower. Utilizing faceting and the curvature of the dome, Ayotte disperses light through a small spot of color in the back of the piece to create the illusory turquoise halo around the flowers. This special tribute to the rose is a testimony to the statement, *"a thing of beauty is a joy forever."*

74. Bouquet with honeybee and spirit, Healing Bouquet Series, lampwork encasement with lampwork, Paul Stankard, dated 1992, diameter 3". Blue forget-me-nots mingle with daisies, ripening blackberries and a pink and blue-striped morning glory in this amazingly life-like bouquet. A bee moving among the blooms adds to the botanical credibility of the piece, hinting at the cycles of nature and the pollination process. On the bottom of the piece, a spirit clings to tendrils of growth, conjuring the myth of the dryad, a mystical being thought to nurture plants.

75. White-rayed wyethia blossoms, lampwork encasement with lampwork, Chris Buzzini, dated 1992, diameter 3 1/16". The daisy has always been associated with prophecy, and even today young girls in love pluck the petals from the flower saying, "he loves me, he loves me not." Chris Buzzini captures the romance of these flowers in this natural portrayal. The repetition of mitre-cuts on the outside of the piece creates an abstract flower shape that frames the overlapping wyethia blossoms and emphasizes the shape of their petals.

76. Blue butterfly, lampwork encasement with lamp-work, Mayauel Ward, dated 1993, diameter 3 3/16".
A blue butterfly flutters up to a bouquet of poppies and pink phlox in this whimsical scene. Ward mixes realism and imagination in this fanciful tribute to the beauty of mother nature.

77. Arizona coral snake, lampwork encasement with lampwork, Gordon Smith, dated 1992, diameter 3 3/8".
Gordon Smith invites viewers to marvel at the hypnotizing coils of the coral snake as it slithers by yucca plants in its natural environment. The brilliant natural coloring of the reptile allows Smith to draw from antique and modern realist traditions at the same time.

78. Double primrose on emerald ground, lampwork encasement with lampwork, Johne Parsley, dated 1993, diameter 2 3/16". Johne Parsley specializes in small-sized paperweights with incredibly fine lampwork designs. Sparkling like a precious jewel, this piece showcases primroses, a classic theme, on an emerald ground.

79. Collaborative piedouche with Warden pears on lace, furnace work with lampwork and millefiori, Johne Parsley with Peter McDougall of Perthshire Paperweights, dated 1993, height 2 13/16", diameter 2 7/8". In this collaborative effort, the artists emphasize they are paying homage to the beauty of pears by placing them on a pedestal. Parsley's lampwork captures the splendor of the fruit as portrayed in the famous Traité des arbres fruitiers by Pierre Jean Francois Turpin, while McDougall's canework heightens the delicacy of this grand presentation.

80. Yellow crimp rose in turquoise-over-white double overlay, lampwork encasement with crimp and lampwork, Charles Kaziun II, ca. 1960–1970, diameter 2 5/16". Charles Kaziun's Millville-type rose was developed over three years of experimentation. He achieved the wonderful dimensionality of the flower with the aid of a crimp, a special tool used to insert glass into the dome of a paperweight. The beautiful overlay is cut with windows which highlight the loveliness of this blossom.

81. Red double clematis in basket, lampwork encasement with lampwork and millefiori, Bob Banford, dated 1984, diameter 3". The inventive use of cutting on the overlay to form a basket is a Banford trademark. A cascade of rich colors, the bouquet is formed with jewel-like precision.

82. Double-tiered pink blossom in frosted crystal, furnace work with torchwork and millefiori, Correia Art Glass, dated 1983, diameter 2 3/4". Correia artisans employed classical lampwork and millefiori techniques to create this Indian rose. The silky, delicate traceries of the flower are formed by placing cupped petals inside each other.

83. MICRO PIEDOUCHE, furnace work with millefiori, Drew Ebelhare, dated 1993, diameter 1 5/16". The diminutive size of this piece adds to its preciousness. Drew Ebelhare outdoes himself with this poetic portrayal of a tiny bouquet of stars.

84. Hollow weight with Giant Panda, furnace work with lampwork, Perthshire Paperweights, dated 1992, diameter 3 1/8". Inside a hollow-blown dome of crystal, a doll-like panda bear munches on eucalyptus leaves. Perthshire captures the priceless charm of this species inside a faceted blue flash overlay.

CONTEMPORARY DESIGNS

85. CHARMED FRAGRANCE, Botanical Series, lampwork encasement with lampwork and lamination, Paul Stankard, dated 1991, 6 7/8" x 5". This extraordinary piece was inspired by the nineteenth-century French botanical painters, whose artistic goal was to lead the viewer from admiration of their portrayal of flowers to contemplation of the plants themselves. Paul Stankard portrays this meadow scene of pink tea roses and blue forget-me-nots with amazing accuracy, transforming hard glass into everything from the fuzz on a bee's back to the flower's delicate petals and stamens. Stankard takes great pains to depict a slice of nature, including the plant's root system, and a cocoon full of yellow larvae below the plant.

86. SPRING MORNING, Confine Series, lampwork encasement with lampwork and lamination, Chris Buzzini, dated 1993, 7 7/8"x 3 7/16". This piece draws inspiration from the famous stanza of William Blake's *Auguries of Innocence:*

> To see a World in a Grain of Sand,
> And a Heaven in a Wild Flower,
> Hold Infinity in the palm of your hand,
> and Eternity in an hour.

Buzzini encases these sentiments in crystal, presenting a tangible vision of the poem with this collection of flowers which will never wilt or fade. Among the life-like flowers in this tribute, one finds lavender-blue asters, pink morning glories, purple lilacs and striped pink apple blossoms. Contemplating the delicately-woven blossoms provides a wonderful release from the pressures of daily life.

87. Hummingbird sculpture with pink morning glory, lampwork encasement with lampwork, Victor Trabucco, dated 1989, approx. 5 3/8" x 4 13/16". A crystal hummingbird searches for nectar in the throat of vibrant pink morning glories in this imaginative portrayal. Trabucco applies lampwork techniques to both the inside and the outside of the weight.

88. DUCKS ON THE POND, lampwork encasement with lampwork, Rick Ayotte, dated 1992, diameter 3 15/16". "I first became fascinated with mallard ducks during family vacations at Back Lake in Pittsburgh, New Hampshire. Sitting on the dock, watching my children feed crackers to the ducks, I was struck by their intricate coloring, and their gentle manner. In this piece, I tried hard to recreate the special magic of watching the ducks on a lake," says Rick Ayotte. He incorporates over fifty different colors into this piece to create the scene of mallard ducks out for a paddle around the pond on a sunny day. The male, female and duckling all display the appropriate coloring of the species. Looking carefully, it is even possible to discern a sheen of pollen on the top of the water.

89. CAT IN THE WINDOW, RAINY AFTERNOON, lampwork encasement with lampwork, millefiori and engraving, Debbie Tarsitano with Max Erlacher, dated 1993, diameter 3 3/8". Debbie Tarsitano captures the sophisticated demure essence of the feline in this charming portrayal, which includes the innovative use of engraving. The cat dozes languidly beneath a curved branch of flowers, each with a Clichy-type rose center. Working from one of Debbie's drawings, former Steuben master engraver Max Erlacher engraved the compelling scene on the back of this weight.

90. Green frog on lily pads, lampwork encasement with lampwork, Jim Donofrio, dated 1993, diameter 3 3/8". Jim Donofrio captures the motion of a frog as it moves across lily pads near a pink water lily. This piece is an astonishing demonstration of Donofrio's ability to breathe life into glass.

91. STARLIGHT BOUQUET, lampwork encasement with lampwork, Ken Rosenfeld, dated 1993, height 3 1/4". Ken Rosenfeld combines inventive design and eye-catching color in this dramatic arrangement of cherries and fantasy flowers. The special cutting on the back of the piece creates the illusion of flowers illuminated by a night sky full of twinkling stars.

92. ANCESTRAL DREAM, Atlantis Series, lampwork encasement with lampwork, Gordon Smith, dated 1993, height 3 1/16", diameter 3 1/2". Gordon Smith draws on the legend of Atlantis in this portrayal of a bottlenose dolphin swimming past sunken columns. While Atlantis may only be a myth, it stands as an exciting metaphor for the ocean's hidden secrets and unknown potential.

*93. Earthlife Sculpture, **lampwork encasement with lampwork**, Delmo Tarsitano, dated 1988, diameter 2 5/16".* In this diorama we find two wolf spiders and a wasp in the midst of blooming prickly pear cactus. Looking inside the crystal evokes the childhood ritual of studying insects inside a mason jar. Tarsitano portrays this nature scene with a child-like fascination and wonder. From certain angles the interior scene is mirrored on the sides of the optically-cut crystal in this piece, an illusion that makes the interior of the piece appear larger than its exterior.

*94. **Magnum compound cranes with Japanese iris flowers, furnace work with torchwork,** Daniel Salazar of Lundberg Studios, dated 1993, diameter 4 11/16".* A pair of feathery white cranes fly over a pond full of white and blue-striped iris blossoms in this awe-inspiring scene. Daniel Salazar utilizes Lundberg Studios' California-style crystal encasement technique to layer the parts of this scene, instilling the weight with a rare dimensionality. The birds' wings, for example, cast a shadow on the green leaves and stems of the flowers. The crane was originally a symbol of vigilance, and through its ability to stay alert the bird has become associated with longevity, good fortune and conjugal fidelity. As legend has it, the crane always carries a stone in one claw so if it begins to nap at an inopportune moment, the sound of the dropped rock will awaken it. In Japanese tradition, a pair of cranes flying in tandem is meant to express good wishes.

*95. **Horned owl on aventurine, furnace work with torchwork and millefiori,** Ed Alexander of Orient and Flume Art Glass, dated 1992, diameter 3 3/4".* Utilizing techniques similar to those found in an antique Baccarat butterfly, Ed Alexander ingeniously employed millefiori canes to produce this charming rendition of the owl. The rich aventurine ground creates the illusion of stars twinkling in the night sky.

96. Yellow-striped green salamander, lampwork encasement with lampwork, Jim Donofrio, dated 1993, diameter 3 3/8". In this portrayal of medieval legend, a gnome rides the back of a salamander while another watches. Jim Donofrio merges folklore with startling realism in this dramatic presentation.

97. Rana Interno Vetrinetta [Frog in Glass Case], lampwork encasement with lampwork, David and Jon Trabucco, dated 1993, diameter 3". Animal weights often impart a sense of impending movement to the viewer, adding a dimension of unfolding drama to the paperweight that is not found in floral sprays. In this piece, the bullfrog's legs are tense, as though it is about to jump right out of the weight. It is easy to imagine it just landed on this patch of dirt as it was being pursued by a little boy.

98. Aquarium, furnace work with torchwork, Steven Lundberg of Lundberg Studios, dated 1993, 2 15/16 x 4 9/16". Exotic angel fish swim near blue jellyfish floating amidst a garden of multicolored seaweed in this dazzling scene. Steven Lundberg has been a key figure in the popularization of marine life portrayals.

99. WORLDWEIGHT, special powdered glass technique, Lundberg Studios, dated 1993, diameter 3 1/2". This innovative and imaginative piece, conceived by Jim Lundberg, captures the beauty and tranquillity of the Earth viewed from space. Lundberg Studios developed a special technique of rolling crystal in powdered glass to create the gorgeous coloring of the weight.

100. SPRING, Monet Series, furnace work with torchwork and millefiori, Peter Raos, dated 1993, height 3 1/4", diameter 3". Inspired by the impressionist paintings of Claude Monet, New Zealand artist Peter Raos produced Spring. This poetic arrangement captures the essence of a field of wildflowers on a breezy spring day.

101. Snowman with tree, lampwork encasement with lampwork, Bobby Banford, dated 1988, diameter 3". A snowman and a bare tree stand in the midst of gently-falling snow. This endearing paperweight conjures vivid personal memories, such as watching snow fall outside your window, or building your first snowman.

*102. B*ɪʀᴄʜ, *furnace work with torchwork, Yaffa Sikorsky-Todd and Jeffrey M. Todd, dated 1992, diameter 3".* This piece, reminiscent of a Japanese water-color landscape, was created by a unique method of "painting" with glass rods. The graceful tree is decorated with hanging vines of millefiori flowers. The scene evokes thoughts of picnics, walks in the woods and secret rendezvous.

103. Bananas on blue ground, furnace work with lampwork, Baccarat, dated 1988, diameter 3 1/4". Ever since Josephine Baker danced at the *Folies Bergèrt* in Paris, the banana has had a profound effect on the French people. This rendition is lively, exotic and dimensional.

104. Running zebras, furnace work with sandblasting, Correia Art Glass, dated 1992, diameter 3". This carousel arrangement of running zebras makes a powerful graphic presentation. Correia artisans sandblasted the surface of a black overlay to create this fascinating surface design.

105. HEART OF THE NIGHT, furnace work with torchwork, David Salazar, dated 1993, approx. diameter 2 5/8". David Salazar charts the movements of lovers under the stars in this Romeo and Juliet-inspired piece. Salazar utilizes the heart-shaped exterior to help portray his theme. Inspired by Juliet's statement about Romeo, *"Take him and cut him out in little stars, and he will make the face of heaven so fine that all the world will be in love with night."*

106. SILVER DREAMER, furnace work and silver electro-forming, Andrew Fote, dated 1993, diameter 3 3/16". Andrew Fote conjures the liberating sensations of the world we enter when we sleep, combining an innovative silver overlay with sparkling crystal in this intriguing display.

107. Abstract blue-veiled candle, furnace work with veiling , Ed Nesteruk, dated 1992, height 4 3/4". Drawing from knowledge gained during seventeen years as a chemical engineer, Ed Nesteruk applies thin coatings of precious metals to crystal to create brilliant translucent veils. In this weight, an abstract candle shape was created using thin layers of silver.

108. Soul in a Cage, cold work and sandblasting, Barry Sautner, dated 1993, diameter 3 11/16". In this piece, we find the crystal figure of a man trapped in a prison so confining it is impossible to move. Sautner's portrayal is so vivid it makes the viewer feel uncomfortable. One of the most evocative pieces in the exhibition, the beauty of this paperweight rests not in its portrayal, but in the message it conveys: *"A soul is meant to wander freely."*

ARTIST BIOGRAPHIES

Rick Ayotte—In the world of paperweights, Rick Ayotte is known as the "bird man" of glass. His fascination with birds goes back to childhood where, in his native Nashua, New Hampshire, he charted migratory bird groups and carved life-size birds out of wood. Since the late 1970s, Ayotte has been making ornithologically accurate paperweights. His skill and artistic expression have now grown to include naturalistic settings that lend reality and depth to the field of birds they surround, and three-dimensional still-life paperweights of incredible realism and complexity. His pieces are part of numerous museum collections, including The Art Institute of Chicago, The Smithsonian Institution and The Bergstrom-Mahler Museum.

Baccarat—The company that is today called Compagnie des Cristalleries de Baccarat, was founded in 1764, under the name Verrerie de Sainte Anne, by Monseigneur de Montmorency-Laval, Bishop of Metz. In 1816, the factory was sold to M. Aimé-Gabriel d'Artigues, who had worked as director of the Saint Louis factory. Under his direction, the glassworks improved rapidly, becoming France's foremost glassworks by 1822. Baccarat produced the most beautiful crystal in the world; the heaviest (because of its 32% lead content), the most refractive, and the most luminous. In 1823 d'Artigues sold the company and it was renamed Compagnie des Cristalleries de Baccarat. In 1846, under the management of Emile Godard, the craftsmen at Baccarat perfected the production of millefiori paperweights. By 1848 exquisite lampwork flowers, bouquets, butterflies and other motifs were also being produced. Paperweight manufacture at Baccarat was a small but significant part of the company's production for almost twenty years, but it gradually faded. In 1953, collector and connoisseur Paul Jokelson suggested that Baccarat experiment with making sulphide paperweights. Their first attempt, which was a piece based on Dwight D. Eisenhower's campaign medal, was unsuccessful. But the experiment proved to the craftsmen that encasing cameos in glass was possible. That same year, the factory produced its first successful contemporary sulphide commemorating the coronation of Queen Elizabeth II of England. The paperweight proved extremely popular and led Baccarat to the production of a long series of sulphides. Because Baccarat had no records of the millefiori technique, it took several years of research and experimentation before they succeeded in producing millefiori pieces in 1957. With the advice and help of Francis Whittemore, Baccarat craftsman Jean Benoit mastered the technique of lampwork style paperweights, and in 1974 began an annual lampwork collection.

Bob Banford and his father Ray Banford, began seriously producing paperweights in a small studio behind their family home in Hammonton, New Jersey in 1971. Banford's classic-style paperweights include lampwork flowers, intricate upright and flat bouquets, bumblebees, dragonflies and salamanders. Ray and Bob's paperweights are a part of many museum collections, including The Smithsonian Institution, The Art Institute of Chicago, The Bergstrom-Mahler Museum, The American Museum of Glass at Wheaton Village and The Corning Museum of Glass.

Bobby Banford—Bobby Lee Sanford married Bob Banford in 1984. She began spending her spare time at the Banford studio learning how to make clear glass animals and ornaments. Shortly thereafter, she began working in the studio full-time creating glass paperweights. Her subjects include floral motifs, undersea designs and holiday scenes.

Ray Banford first became intrigued by the idea of making paperweights after visiting the workshop of Adolph Macho, an elderly Czechoslovakian glass craftsman in Vineland, New Jersey. Ray had worked as an antique dealer for many years and often did business with paperweight makers Pete Lewis and John Choko. A visit to The Corning Museum of Glass served as further inspiration. In 1971, Ray and his son, Bob, began making paperweights of their own. Ray's weights include bouquets of lampwork flowers, as well as paperweight buttons and pendants. Occasionally, Ray and Bob Banford have produced "combination weights," in which lampwork elements made by both artists are encased within a single weight.

Chris Buzzini—In 1949, Christopher Lee Buzzini was born in Yosemite National Park. The magnificent natural beauty of his birthplace was to have a great influence on his future career, giving him a strong connection to nature and a love of color and detail. Buzzini first set up a glass studio in his home, where he could experiment on his own. In 1972, he became a small-interest partner in the newly formed art glass studio of Orient & Flume. From there he went on to work at several prominent art glass studios in California, including Lundberg Studios and Correia Art Glass. He also had the rare opportunity to work with a patron, Gaylord Evey, who was instrumental in setting up a studio for him in New Jersey. In the fall of 1986, Buzzini set up his own studio in southern California where he could be free to formulate and create the type of detail and realism that his personal aesthetic demanded. From that moment, he began making the superb botanically accurate weights for which he is now known.

Clichy—Very little recorded information has been found on the third of the three great French factories—Clichy-la-Garenne. Founded by Messrs. Rouyer and Maës, even the founding date and original location are uncertain. Two possibilities are 1837 at Billancourt, or 1838 at Sèvres. It is known that shortly after the business was formed, the operation was moved to Clichy, which is now a suburb of Paris. At first the factory produced inexpensive glass for export, but by the 1840s both Saint Louis and Baccarat were concerned about the company's rapid growth and the improving quality of its glassware. As early as 1844, Clichy exhibited with Baccarat and Saint Louis in Paris, where the young company's exquisite colored and overlay crystal was highly praised.

Correia Art Glass was founded by Steven Correia in 1974. The studio has become world famous for its art nouveau and art deco designs, iridescent color and exceptional quality,

Jim Donofrio applies skills he learned creating wood and bronze sculpture to his realistic paperweights. Paul Stankard introduced Donofrio to the paperweight art form in 1981, and he spent eight years as Stankard's assistant, acquiring many of the skills he needed to make paperweights. Donofrio likes to portray scenes that focus attention on specific areas of nature, detailing wonders that are often overlooked. Donofrio's pieces are included in the collections of The Corning Museum of Glass, The Bergstrom-Mahler Museum and the Birks Museum.

Drew Ebelhare is one of two paperweight makers in the United States devoted to the production of millefiori weights. Ebelhare, who has been working with hot glass since the early eighties, says his main source of inspiration is the great French antiques, which he attempts to interpret in his own style.

Andrew Fote divides his time between working as a teacher at the New Orleans School of Glass Works and making paperweights. When he is not teaching, he lives in Seattle, Washington. Fote has a classical art background which includes studying art at the Academia in Florence, Italy. He is fascinated by the human figure and includes it in much of his work. He received his glass training at the Pilchuk Glass School, and has studied with many of the world's most famous glass artists.

Randall Grubb was first introduced to hot glass in the art department at the University of Southern California. He fell in love with the hot glass process for its seemingly unlimited potential. As part of his study, he worked for Correia Art Glass in southern California as an equipment builder. Such in-depth exposure to the many facets of hot glass gave Grubb tremendous experience. It also gave him his introduction to paperweights. At the studio he met paperweight artist Chris Buzzini, who greatly influenced his future career, giving him guidance and training in the art of making paperweights. His first weights were made with torchwork procedures, but he found they lacked the three-dimensional quality he wanted. Soon he began experimenting with lampwork techniques. Grubb currently designs and creates his own line of lampwork paperweights in his Oregon studio. Because he pulls his own canes to obtain exactly the right shades, his use of color is exceptionally delicate and satisfying. Many of his weights contain full, colorful bouquets with high domes. His bouquets have become increasingly more complex in color, design and size. He is also one of the few artists using the complicated overlay and double overlay techniques, often with special cutting to highlight his original designs.

Charles Kaziun (1919–1992), one of the pioneers of paperweight making, began working in 1939 to rediscover the lost techniques of the French glass factories. His work includes a wide range of millefiori, lampwork and crimp flower paperweights and related items. Kaziun produced excellent spaced and patterned millefiori on colored grounds which were often flecked with gold. He also perfected a swirling latticinio cane and a brilliant two-sided torsade. Over the years, Kaziun created a wide range of flower weights, incorporating the pansy, hibiscus, dogwood, convolvulus and, in one of his most popular pieces, a miniature spider lily. His roses, which are smaller than their Millville counterparts, are highly valued by collectors today. Kaziun's paperweights are a part of many museum collections, including The Art Institute of Chicago, The Bergstrom-Mahler Museum and The Smithsonian Institution.

Lundberg Studios was founded by James Lundberg (1948-1992) in Davenport, California in 1973. In 1974, Lundberg Studios began producing an entirely new form of paperweight, using a technique called the California Paperweight Style (or torchwork). These pieces combined two antique styles—the art nouveau "icepick" technique and lampwork. Utilizing more sophisticated canes, layering and pre-lampworked inserts, the technique has become a major new direction in paperweight making. This evolutionary process is the culmination of almost twenty years of development and is mainly the work of Steven Lundberg and Daniel Salazar, with notable contributions early on by James Lundberg, Mark Cantor, David Salazar and Chris Buzzini. Lundberg Studios' clear-encased weights with floral, bird, butterfly and seascape motifs have marked the emergence of a new form of paperweight.

Mount Washington Glass Company—In 1837, Deming Jarves founded the Mount Washington Glass Company in South Boston. He started the company for his son George, who was twelve years old at the time. Unfortunately, George died in 1850 at the age of twenty-five. After the death of Deming Jarves in 1869, the firm changed hands many times. Not much is known about the paperweights made there, but it is known that master glassblower Nicholas Lutz worked at Mount Washington between 1892 and 1895, perhaps creating many of the unusual and outstanding   magnum paperweights and plaques for which the company is known.

Ed Nesteruk of Pittsburgh, Pennsylvania spent seventeen years as a research engineer devoted to finding new methods of coloring hot glass surfaces. He founded his own glass studio in 1980. His vast knowledge of coloration has proven to be his trademark. Several patents have been issued in his name, all related to glass coatings. Nesteruk's paperweights feature thin glass veils with a light, gossamer quality.

New England Glass Company (NEGC), also referred to simply as "Cambridge Glass," came into being in 1818. It grew out of the purchase at public auction of two Cambridge firms: the Boston Porcelain & Glass Company and Emmet, Fisher & Flowers. Four partners, among them Deming Jarves, who became general manager, incorporated in 1818 as the New England Glass Company of Lechmere Point, East Cambridge, Massachusetts.

The company soon became one of the leading flint glass producers in the country. Workers there began experimenting with decorative glassware and their extensive product line included every variety of plain, engraved and pressed glass. By 1850, the factory's work force had grown to 500 men, working around the clock. The New England Glass Company produced paperweights from about 1850 to 1880. Its first known weight was a piece commemorating the Great Exhibition of 1851, which featured intaglio portraits of Queen Victoria and Prince Albert.

Orient and Flume Art Glass—In 1972, Douglas Boyd and David Hopper opened a small glassblowing studio in Chico, California. The two artists, who had taken part in some of the earliest college glassblowing classes offered on the West Coast, received master's degrees in glass from San Jose State University. The studio has grown from a two-person operation to a glassworks with a staff of twenty people, a size that is still small enough to allow each artist the chance to work and create as an individual. The company developed its reputation producing brilliant iridescent glass paperweights with art nouveau motifs and elaborate surface decoration. When Boyd and Hopper began experimenting with formulas, iridescent glass had not been produced for almost half a century. Early paperweights were made using the technique of torchwork, where molten threads or dots are applied to the surface of a piece and then manipulated to create a pattern. Later weights include clear-encased lampwork designs.

Pantin—In 1850, E. S. Monot established a glassworks at La Villette, near Paris, under the name of Monot et Cie. After moving the company and opening a showroom in Paris, the glass factory moved again to Pantin, No. 84, rue de Paris. By 1873, Monot had been joined by his son and by M. F. Stumpf. The title of the firm was changed at that time to Monot, père et fils, et Stumpf. The Pantin glassworks produced glass tubes and chemical glassware, as well as fine crystal table glasses, tumblers, perfume bottles and chandeliers.

Parabelle Glass—Husband and wife Gary and Doris Scrutton of Parabelle Glass in Portland, Oregon represent one of two studios in the United States concentrating exclusively on the production of millefiori paperweights. Gary first began working with glass in the 1950s. He started as an apprentice after high school, learning general glassworking techniques such as beveling, etching and mirror silvering. He later started his own studio which specialized in stained glass. In 1983, he sold the business to his two sons, and he and Doris set up a small studio in the back of their home. They began making millefiori weights, which, Gary says, hold so much more mystery for him. With only the most general information available, Gary spent the first year in his new studio experimenting with the making of glass and the development of techniques. He worked diligently to overcome problems involving equipment, design and the making of colors and canes. In contrast to many studio artists, Gary makes all his own colors, purchasing his raw materials from a local supplier. He has also developed a highly sophisticated glass studio with computers regulating the temperatures of the furnace and the glass formulas.

Johne Parsley began producing paperweights in 1983 at the age of 66. He began glassblowing in 1939, and his pieces exhibit his years of experience. Parsley specializes in extremely delicate miniature-sized weights with fruits and flowers. His pieces can be found in numerous museum collections, including The Bergstrom-Mahler Museum, The Corning Museum of Glass and The American Museum of Glass at Wheaton Village.

Perthshire Paperweights was founded by the late Stuart Drysdale, a country lawyer and businessman, who became intrigued with the idea of creating paperweights equal to those made during the classic period. In 1968, Drysdale and the master glassblowers of Strathearn Glass, left that company and formed Perthshire Paperweights. For the first two years, the operation was located in an old schoolhouse that had been converted into a makeshift factory. In 1971, Perthshire Paperweights moved into a newly constructed modern factory on the outskirts of Crieff. They are now one of the few factory-size operations in the world devoted exclusively to making paperweights and paperweight-related items. About three-quarters of a ton of glass is now produced each week at Perthshire. The factory employs about thirty craftspeople, who work together designing and producing paperweights. Millefiori and lampwork designs are created by individual glassworkers, who are encouraged to experiment with glass.

Peter Raos is New Zealand's most famous glass artist. Former president of The New Zealand Society of Artists in Glass, Raos also founded The Hot Glass Company in Devonport. His pieces have been exhibited in numerous museums and galleries, including The Christchurch Museum and The Aukland War Memorial Museum.

Ken Rosenfeld specializes in detailed lampwork designs exhibiting the bold colors of traditional French paperweights. His pieces include a variety of flowers, floral bouquets, fruit and vegetables. Rosenfeld's work reflects his skill as a craftsman as well as his accomplishments as an artist and designer. What interests Rosenfeld most is the color and the liveliness of the design. While quality and composition are important to Rosenfeld, his main focus is on the innovative use of color. This is apparent in both his interior motifs and translucent color grounds. Cristalleries de Saint Louis was established in 1767, three years after the Cristalleries de Baccarat. Originally named Verrerie Royale de Saint Louis for King Saint Louis of France, the factory was established in the Munzthal forest in the Lorraine region of France. It was an excellent location due to the abundance of wood, sand and potash. In 1829 the company adopted a new name: Compagnie des Cristalleries de Saint Louis. Two years later, Saint Louis and Baccarat decided to sell their glassware through a retail operation and entered into a joint agreement with the firm of Launay, Hautin et Cie. in Paris. Because of its ranking just behind Baccarat, Saint Louis tried to attract customers by developing new lines of articles. Thus it is not surprising that it was the first French factory to show an interest in the production of paperweights. One of its first millefiori weights was dated 1845, and by 1848 Saint Louis was producing a wide range of lampwork pieces as well. In 1953, after a lapse of eighty-six years, Cristalleries de Saint Louis once again began making paperweights. The initial prompting came from Paul Jokelson, who at the same time had encouraged paperweight production at Baccarat and Cristal d'Albret. Paul Gossman, an energetic young glassmaker at Saint Louis, consulted with the older workers at the factory, then conducted test after test to rediscover the forgotten millefiori, lampwork and sulphide techniques. It was not until 1970 that Saint Louis made a commitment to produce paperweights on a regular basis. The company also produces a number of paperweight-related items, such as handcoolers, candlesticks, newel posts, perfume bottles and pen holders.

David Salazar watched the fascinating process of glassblowing for the first time in 1972. As Mark Cantor, James Lundberg's partner at the time, explained the process, Salazar projected what he would do if given the chance. With a limited background in scientific glass work and a strong desire to learn the magic art of blowing glass, he became an apprentice at Lundberg Studios. From the beginning Salazar's emphasis was in decorating. So in 1973, when Larry Selman suggested he concentrate on paperweights, the door was opened. The early days flew by with a seemingly endless work load and a lot of after-hours experimentation. In the course of that year he combined his experience in scientific glass work and conventional glass methods with the new techniques he had learned to create images that had never before been made.

Barry Sautner, of Lansdale, Pennsylvania, began creating diatreta and insculpture paperweights in 1984 while working at the Vandermark/Merritt Glass Studios. Diatreta is an extremely difficult and unusual process accomplished entirely by sandblasting on cold glass. The term translates from Greek as "openwork" or "lattice-work." Sautner also uses a sandblasting technique, called insculpture, that is his alone. By working through small holes in the base, he can create three-dimensional flowers and leaves in the center of the crystal. In 1986 Barry Sautner opened Sautner Cameo Studio. Sautner's subjects range from the unusual and controversial to the sublimely beautiful. Sautner's pieces are part of numerous museum collections, including The Bergstrom-Mahler Museum, The Newark Museum, The Museum of American Glass, The Birks Museum and The Corning Museum of Glass.

Gordon Smith, an avid scuba diver and naturalist, is one of the acknowledged masters of paperweight-making. His complex paperweights display his love for the natural beauty of the sea and desert. Smith's pieces can be seen in museums around the world, including The American Museum of Glass at Wheaton Village, The Bergstrom-Mahler Museum, Christchurch Museum in New Zealand, and the Royal Ontario Museum in Canada.

Paul Stankard of Mantua, New Jersey, is perhaps the most prolific and accomplished paperweight artist working today. His skills have developed over thirty years of working in glass. Stankard's work features botanically-accurate glass flowers, focusing on detail, exact coloration, and the life cycle of the plant. He has a love of wildflowers and many of his paperweights have intricate root systems that are detailed with as much care as the colorful blooms above the ground.

His love of nature has most recently translated into poetry, which is intended to interpret the voice of a flower, heightening the insight to his sculpted glass botanicals. Throughout his career, Stankard has continued to expand the limits of the paperweight as an art form. He has conducted many studies, experimenting with color and composition, to achieve his own personal interpretation of nature. During his career, Stankard has explored the limits of glass as an artistic medium. His extensive background in glass technology and his curiosity and drive as an artist have led him to create some of the finest and most original work being done today. His pieces are part of numerous museum collections, including The Cleveland Art Museum, The Boston Fine Arts Museum, The Royal Ontario Museum, The Smithsonian Institution, The Corning Museum of Glass, The Victoria and Albert Museum, The Louvre, The Bergstrom-Mahler Museum, The American Museum of Glass at Wheaton Village and The Chrysler Museum.

Yaffa Sikorsky-Todd and Jeffrey M. Todd have been working together for 13 years producing pieces incorporating their unique style of torchwork imagery. All of the colors and crystal glasses in their paperweights are melted in their studio, using formulas that Yaffa developed over the last sixteen years. They exhibit their pieces nationally and internationally in museums around the world including The Chrysler Museum in Virginia, The Bergstrom-Mahler Museum in Wisconsin, The American Museum of Glass at Wheaton Village, Glassmuseum Ebeltoft in Denmark, The Kestner Museum in Germany, The Haaretz Museum in Israel, Glassmuseum Frauenau in Germany, The North Carolina Museum of History, The Asheville Museum of Art and The Mint Museum in North Carolina.

Debbie Tarsitano and her father, Delmo Tarsitano, saw their first glass paperweight at an auction in 1971. The purchase of that first paperweight and the enthusiasm it engendered led them to experiment with glass on their own. Delmo had taken a short course in glassmaking, and Debbie could make simple glass animals. Thus, with a borrowed torch and glass, they set up their first studio in 1976. Since those early days, with much trial and error, good instincts, and indomitable spirits, the two have become highly regarded paperweight artists. Debbie's paperweights have been greatly influenced by her background in painting. She graduated from Hofstra University with a degree in art and painting. Her study of painting has inspired the style, color, and design of her paperweights. Each paperweight is an individual work of art. She sometimes works in collaboration with the master engraver Max Erlacher, who worked at Steuben Glass for many years. Tarsitano paperweights are part of numerous museum collections, including The Corning Museum of Glass, The Smithsonian Institution, The Bergstrom-Mahler Museum, The Art Institute of Chicago, The Royal Ontario Museum, The Flint Institute of Glass and The Museum of Contemporary Crafts.

Delmo Tarsitano (1921-1991) was born in northern Italy and grew up in the New York City area. He produced his first successful paperweight in 1976. Three years later, he and his daughter Debbie began making paperweights full-time. Tarsitano is renowned for his fruit weights and salamander weights. He is also known for his "Earthlife" weights—realistic presentations of spiders in their own natural environments. These display complete mastery of the technical aspects of lampwork, with his grounds, creatures and delicate flowers. With consummate skill, he employed optical cutting to enhance each lifelike scene.

Jon and David Trabucco—In the Trabucco household, glassworking is a trade that has been passed on from father to son. Following in the European apprenticeship tradition, brothers David and Jon began working at an early age under their father, the renowned glass artist Victor Trabucco. Today, both men possess finely-honed glass working skills. As apprentices, the twins became heirs to secrets that had taken Victor over twenty years to discover. Now, David and Jon are respected artists in their own right, working at their father's studio producing their own paperweights and collaborating with their father on special projects.

Victor Trabucco of Buffalo, New York, first became interested in glass in 1974. He began his career in glassmaking as a sculptor, quickly receiving award-winning recognition for his work. In 1977, after examining a number of French paperweights, he began experimenting with paperweight making. He was fascinated with the possibilities inherent in melding delicate lampwork arrangements in solid crystal. After a year of trial and error he successfully mastered the technique. Since then, Trabucco has created hundreds of lampwork paperweight designs. Early on, the focus of his work became to overcome the technical problems of working with glass in order to allow more latitude for artistic expression. Victor Trabucco's obsession with hard work and experimentation is evident in the distinctive quality of his work. His pieces contain some of the most dramatic and vividly three-dimensional lampwork being created today. Trabucco's pieces are included in several museum collections, including The Corning Museum of Glass, The Art Institute of Chicago, The American Museum of Glass at Wheaton Village, The Bergstrom-Mahler Museum and The Birks Museum.

Mayauel Ward is a master glass artist at Abelman Art Glass in Southern California. His solo efforts include butterflies, salamanders, orchids and wildflowers created with amazing skill and delicacy.

BIBLIOGRAPHY

Annual Bulletin of the Paperweight Collectors' Association. New York: Paperweight Collectors' Association, 1955– .

Boore, J. P. Articles on paperweights in *Hobbies—The Magazine for Collectors;* January 1958 through November 1966.

Casper, Geraldine J. *Glass Paperweights of The Bergstrom-Mahler Museum.* Richmond, Virginia: U.S. Historical Society Press, 1989.

——————————. *Glass Paperweights in The Art Institute of Chicago.* Chicago, Illinois: The Art Institute of Chicago, 1991.

Catalogues of paperweight sales at Christie's, London; Sotheby's, London and New York; L. H. Selman Ltd., Santa Cruz, California.

Dunlop, Paul H. *The Jokelson Collection of Antique Cameo Incrustation.* Phoenix, Arizona: Papier Presse, 1991.

Elville, E. M. *Paperweights and other Glass Curiosities.* 2nd ed. London: Spring Books, 1967.

Flora in Glass: Paperweights by Paul J. Stankard. London: Spink & Son Ltd., 1981.

Hollister, Paul, Jr. *The Encyclopedia of Glass Paperweights.* New York: Clarkson N. Potter, Bramhall House, 1969.

——————————. *Glass Paperweights of the New-York Historical Society.* New York: Clarkson N. Potter, 1974.

Hollister, Paul and Dwight P. Lanmon. *Paperweights: "Flowers which clothe the meadows".* Corning, New York: The Corning Museum of Glass, 1978.

Ingold, Gérard. *The Art of the Paperweight—Saint Louis.* Santa Cruz, California: Paperweight Press, 1981.

Jargstorf, Sibylle. *Paperweights.* West Chester, Pennsylvania: Schiffer Publishing Ltd., 1991.

Jokelson, Paul. *One Hundred of the Most Important Paperweights.* Privately published, 1966.

——————————. *Sulphides: The Art of Cameo Incrustation.* New York: Thomas A. Nelson, 1968.

Jokelson, Paul and Dena Tarshis. *Baccarat: Paperweights and Related Glass 1820–1860.* Santa Cruz, California: Paperweight Press, 1990.

Kulles, George N. *Identifying Antique Paperweights—Lampwork.* Santa Cruz, California: Paperweight Press, 1987.

——————————. *Identifying Antique Paperweights—Millefiori.* Santa Cruz, California: Paperweight Press, 1985.

Mackay, James. *Glass Paperweights.* New York: Viking Press, 1973.

Paperweight News. Santa Cruz, California: Paperweight Press, 1975– .

Rossi, Sara. *A Collector's Guide to Paperweights.* Secaucus, New Jersey: Wellfleet Press, 1990.

Selman, Lawrence H. *All About Paperweights.* Santa Cruz, California: Paperweight Press, 1992.

——————————. *The Art of the Paperweight—Perthshire.* Santa Cruz, California: Paperweight Press, 1983.

——————————. *Collectors' Paperweights—Price Guide and Catalogue.* Santa Cruz, California: Paperweight Press, 1979, 1981, 1983, 1986.

——————————. *The Art of the Paperweight.* Santa Cruz, California: Paperweight Press, 1988.

Selman, Lawrence H. and Linda Pope-Selman. *Paperweights for Collectors.* Santa Cruz, California: Paperweight Press, 1975.